DECADES OF THE
20TH
CENTURY

1980s

ELDORADO INK

DECADES OF THE 20TH CENTURY

1900s

1910s

1920s

1930s

1940s

1950s

1960s

1970s

1980s

1990s

DECADES OF THE
20TH CENTURY

1980s

ELDORADO INK

Published by Eldorado Ink
2099 Lost Oak Trail
Prescott, AZ 86303
www.eldoradoink.com

Milan Bobek, Editor
Judith C. Callomon, Historical consultant
Samuel J. Patti, Consulting editor

Printed and bound in Slovenia

Publisher Cataloging Data
1980s / [Milan Bobek, editor].
        p. cm. -- (Decades of the 20th century)
      Includes index.
      Summary: This volume, arranged chronologically, presents
key events that have shaped the decade, from significant political
occurrences to details of daily life.
      ISBN 1-932904-08-5
      1. Nineteen eighties   2. History, Modern--20th century--
Chronology   3. History, Modern--20th century--Pictorial works
I. Bobek, Milan   II. Title: Nineteen eighties   III. Series
        909.82/8--dc22

Picture research and photography by Anne Hobart Lang and Rolf
Lang of AHL Archives. Additional research by Heritage Picture
Collection, London.

CONTENTS

THE GLOBAL VILLAGE

The 1980s see countries of the world coming closer, largely through growing awareness of environmental destruction. Poverty and famine in Africa wake the world's conscience as the gap between rich and poor widens. However, discovery of a hole in the ozone layer and nuclear fallout from Chernobyl prove that pollution affects all equally. Politically, the decade sees monumental changes as the INF Treaty is signed, the Berlin Wall comes down, and the Cold War ends.

OPPOSITE: Live Aid, the rock concert that raises over $60 million for famine relief.

1980–1989

KEY EVENTS OF THE DECADE

- IRAN–IRAQ WAR
- THE FALKLANDS CONFLICT
- CIVIL WARS IN CENTRAL AMERICA
- CHERNOBYL
- LIVE AID AND FAMINE RELIEF
- INF TREATY
- IRANGATE
- SOVIET BLOC BREAKS UP
- COLD WAR ENDS

- ORGAN TRANSPLANTS
- AIDS EPIDEMIC
- SPACE SHUTTLE AND SPACE LAB LAUNCHED
- OZONE HOLE DISCOVERED
- COMPACT DISCS
- POSTMODERNISM

WORLD POPULATION: 4,450 MILLION

SOLIDARITY AND WAR

Independent trade unions are recognized in Poland and begin to change the country. Iraq invades neighboring Iran, sparking off war between the two countries. Former film star Ronald Reagan wins the U.S. presidential election for the Republican party. Princess Beatrix becomes queen of the Netherlands. U.S. attempt to rescue hostages in Tehran fails. A new craze for health and fitness sweeps through the United States and Europe. President Tito of Yugoslavia dies and John Lennon is assassinated by a crazed fan.

1980

Feb	13	Winter Olympics are held at Lake Placid, New York
Apr	18	Rhodesia gains legal independence as Zimbabwe
	25	U.S. attempt to rescue hostages in Tehran ends in disaster
	29	Director Alfred Hitchcock, the master of suspense, dies at age 80
May	4	President Tito of Yugoslavia dies aged 88
	18	Mount St. Helens volcano erupts in Washington
July	19	The 22nd Olympic Games open in Moscow
Aug	31	Independent trade unions are recognized in Poland
Sep	22	Iraq invades Iran

Nov	4	Republican Ronald Reagan wins the U.S. presidential election
Dec	8	Former Beatle John Lennon is shot dead outside his home in New York City

ABOVE: Public grief after former Beatle John Lennon is shot dead in New York City

ABOVE: The coronation of Queen Beatrix of the Netherlands in Amsterdam's Nieuwe Kerk; her husband Prince Claus looks on.

IRAN–IRAQ WAR

Profiting from disorder in Iran, Iraq invades neighboring Iran in an attempt to gain the strategic Shatt al-Arab waterway to the Persian Gulf. During the eight year war that follows, Iraq employs chemical weapons and both sides fire ballistic missiles at major cities. Iraq also launches anti-ship missile attacks against tankers shipping oil from Iran. In 1988, Iran accepts a U.N. sponsored cease-fire.

FAILED RESCUE

In a rescue attempt nicknamed "Operation Eagle Claw," the United States sends men from Delta Force 200 miles into Iran to rescue the hostages being held at the U.S. embassy in Tehran. At a refuelling operation in the desert, there is an equipment failure. The force withdraws but the airplane crashes into a tanker aircraft causing the death of eight Americans and injury to others.

ZIMBABWE

After the collapse of the rebel white-only government in Rhodesia, Britain agrees to a new multiracial constitution for the country and grants its last African colony independence as Zimbabwe. Robert Mugabe (b. 1924) becomes prime minister of the new country.

TITO DIES

Yugoslav president Josip Tito dies. His death leads to an eight man collective presidency. Tensions soon begin to emerge between Serbs and Croats in the country.

BEATRIX BECOMES QUEEN

In the Netherlands, Queen Beatrix (b. 1938) takes the throne after her mother, Queen Juliana, abdicates.

HEALTH — THE NEW FASHION

Health clubs and gyms open all over America, Britain, and Europe, offering electronic running machines, classes in aerobic exercise, and dance exercise, to cater to the desire for fitness. The trend influences fashions and cosmetic products.

POLISH SOLIDARITY

After two months of strikes and demonstrations against the government, independent trade unions are recognized in Poland in an agreement between Lech Walesa (b. 1943), strike leader in the Lenin shipyard in Gdansk, and the Polish government. The Solidarity union is formally registered in October.

REAGAN ELECTED PRESIDENT

Ronald Reagan (1911–2004) wins the U.S. presidential election for the Republicans, defeating incumbent president Jimmy Carter. He reverses the consensus politics of his predecessor and begins an arms buildup against the Soviets, working closely with the British government led by Margaret Thatcher.

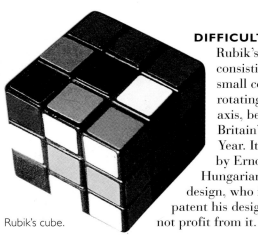

Rubik's cube.

DIFFICULT CUBE
Rubik's cube, a game consisting of 26 small colored cubes rotating on a central axis, becomes Britain's Toy of the Year. It was invented by Erno Rubik, a Hungarian professor of design, who failed to patent his design so he did not profit from it.

AMADEUS
A new play by English dramatist Peter Shaffer (b. 1926) has opened. *Amadeus* tells the story of Mozart and his alleged murder by "rival" composer Salieri. The play courts controversy with its frank portrayal of the earthy, scatological side of Mozart's character.

MOUNT ST. HELENS ERUPTS
The volcano Mount St. Helens in Washington erupts, having been inactive since 1857. The explosion measures 4.1 on the Richter scale. It destroys all life in an area of 154 square miles and kills at least eight people.

BELOW: The force is still with us when *The Empire Strikes Back*, crewed by the same heroes, is released three years after *Star Wars*.

MOSCOW OLYMPICS
Once again politics and sport mix at the Olympic Games. The United States leads a boycott, which includes West Germany and Kenya, in protest at the Soviet Union's invasion of Afghanistan. Competitive highlights include the achievements of British athletes Seb Coe and Steve Ovett on the track, and Soviet gymnast Alexander Ditiatin's perfect 10 in the vault.

SOLAR MAX IS LAUNCHED
Solar Max, the U.S. Solar Maximum Mission Observatory, is launched to record events during a period of sunspot activity.

BYKER DEVELOPMENT
A groundbreaking housing development is created in Newcastle, England. Its importance lies in the fact that it involves the future residents in the design of the building. Members of Ralph Erskine's architectural practice live on site to ensure they are accessible to the future tenants.

SOLAR POWERED FLIGHT
The *Gossamer Penguin* makes the first flight of a solar-powered aircraft in California. The power is obtained from panels of solar electric cells.

WINTER OLYMPICS
The 13th Winter Olympics in Lake Placid witness the first use of artificial snow. American skater Eric Heiden takes five speed skating golds.

ICELAND GAINS WOMAN PRESIDENT

Vigdís Finnbogadóttir (b. 1930) is elected president of Iceland. She wins a little over a third of the vote and defeats three male rivals to become the world's first democratically elected woman president.

BORG WINS FIFTH TITLE

Swedish tennis star Björn Borg (b. 1956) claims his fifth Wimbledon tennis title in a row, beating John McEnroe in the final.

RIGHT: Swedish ace Björn Borg on his way to another Wimbledon win.

JEAN-PAUL SARTRE
(1905–1980)

French existentialist philosopher and writer, Jean-Paul Sartre has died. During World War II, he was a member of the Resistance. A Marxist, he founded, with Simone de Beauvoir, the left-wing journal *Les Temps Modernes* and was known as one of the intellectuals of Left Bank Paris cafe society. His most important philosophical work is *Being and Nothingness* (1943) and his fictional writings include the trilogy *Roads to Freedom* (1945–1949). During the events of May 1968, Sartre was once more out on the streets of Paris supporting student and worker rebellion. Recently, he has suffered from ill-health and near blindness.

BELOW: An infrared photograph taken from a NASA U-2 aircraft showing Mount St. Helens two years before it erupts.

ABOVE: U.S. golfer Jack Nicklaus (b. 1940), the "Golden Bear," confirms his position as one of golf's greatest players.

ABOVE: Ayatollah Khomeini, charismatic fundamentalist leader of Iran, has many supporters for his return to conservative values.

ABOVE: Josip Tito, president of Yugoslavia, and his wife.

JOSIP TITO (BORN JOSIP BROZ) (1892–1980)

President Tito of Yugoslavia, who became head of the Yugoslav Communist party in 1937 and has been the country's leader since the postwar establishment of the new Federal Republic in 1945, has died. Viewed by Stalin as a revisionist, he pursued a policy of liberalism. Although he has been president for life since 1974, he has established a rotating leadership during recent years. The country's future without his leadership is uncertain.

NEW DIRECTION IN THE MOVIES

The late 1970s and early 1980s see the rise of a new generation of young director-producers whose work helps the cinema to recover from the blow inflicted on it by television. Large-scale action films, blockbusters, and science fiction sagas follow, and special effects almost take over as the stars of the films. Audiences flock back to the big screen.

ABOVE: Francis Ford Coppola, enigmatic director most famous for his Mafia-based *Godfather* series.

ABOVE: Michael Cimino directs Robert de Niro on the set of *The Deer Hunter* (1978), the film that makes his name.

ABOVE: Golden boy Steven Spielberg, creator of *Jaws*, *Close Encounters of the Third Kind*, *ET*, and the *Indiana Jones* trilogy.

ABOVE: A scene from Star Wars, the film that launches George Lucas' career as a director.

ABOVE: Douglas Trumball, the special effects mastermind behind many science fiction films and the director of *Silent Running* (1972).

AIDS IS A NEW KILLER

Iran releases the U.S. hostages after 444 days in captivity. Unrest increases in Poland and martial law is declared. François Mitterand is elected the first socialist president of France. President Sadat of Egypt is assassinated. France's new high-speed train reaches speeds of more than 186 miles per hour. A new disease, AIDS, is identified and the first successful heart-lung transplant takes place.

OPPOSITE: Prime Minister Margaret Thatcher meets French president François Mitterand.

1981

Jan	1	Greece joins the European Community (EC)
	20	U.S. hostages released from Tehran
Feb	23	Civil Guards storm Spanish Cortes (parliament) in abortive coup attempt
Mar	30	President Reagan is shot by John Hinckley, Jr. while leaving a D.C. hotel
Apr	12	American reusable space shuttle makes its first flight
May	5	IRA activist Bobby Sands dies from a hunger strike in Northern Ireland
	10	François Mitterand becomes the first socialist president of France
	13	Pope John Paul II is shot and wounded in St. Peter's Square
July	29	Royal wedding of Prince Charles and Lady Diana Spencer, United Kingdom

Oct	6	President Sadat of Egypt is assassinated by Egyptian soldiers
Dec	13	Martial law is declared in Poland and seven striking coal miners are killed

ABOVE: President Anwar Sadat of Egypt, who is assassinated this year.

ABOVE: American writer Susan Sontag is one of a group of Western intellectuals invited to tour Communist China.

ABOVE: Delegates from the States and U.S.S.R. meet in Geneva to discuss the limitation of intermediate nuclear forces in Europe.

ABOVE: Oil rigs begin to reap the rich harvest of North Sea oil.

ABOVE: American composer Samuel Barber, best known for his *Adagio*, dies.

UNREST IN POLAND

In Poland, the Communist government hands over power to the army under General Jaruzelski (b. 1923) who becomes prime minister. He introduces some reforms in April to placate the independent trade union Solidarity, which is leading a general strike. Following demonstrations against food shortages and unrest throughout the country, he introduces martial law in December after pressure from the Soviet Union. He curtails all civil liberties and arrests Solidarity leader Lech Walesa. Solidarity is banned in October 1982.

ATTEMPTED COUP

Right-wing members of the paramilitary Civil Guard storm the Cortes, the Spanish parliament, and attempt to overthrow the government. King Juan Carlos dons a military uniform and instructs the army, which appears to support the coup, to rally behind the democratic government. The government quickly purges the army of former Franco supporters.

MITTERAND BECOMES PRESIDENT

François Mitterand (1916–1996) becomes the first socialist president of France when he wins the presidential election, defeating the incumbent centrist Valéry Giscard d'Estaing. Mitterand's Socialist Party wins a landslide in the general election held in June; the new government includes three Communist ministers.

SADAT ASSASSINATED

Egyptian president Anwar Sadat is assassinated at a military parade by an Islamic extremist protesting against the peace deal with Israel. Sadat is succeeded by Vice President Hosni Mubarak (b. 1928).

HOSTAGES RELEASED

The last 52 hostages are released from the U.S. embassy in Iran, where they have been held by followers of the Ayatollah, moments after Reagan is sworn into office.

GREECE JOINS EC

The newly democratic Greece becomes the tenth nation to be admitted to the European Union.

JAILED HUNGER STRIKER WINS ELECTION

IRA activist Bobby Sands wins the Fermanagh and South Tyrone by-election in Northern Ireland, defeating the Unionists by a clear majority. Bobby Sands, who is on a hunger strike in prison, dies a month later.

HIGH-SPEED TRAIN

In February, France's new TGV (*train à grande vitesse*, or high-speed train) begins a regular service between Paris and Lyon. It sets a world speed record of 236 mph. To reach such speeds, the TGV has specially built tracks with steeply banked curves.

LEFT: April sees the launch of the first space shuttle, a reusable vehicle that can orbit the Earth and return under its own power.

ABOVE: Modern art in a modern setting. Alexander Calder's stable *Flamingo* outside the Federal Center in Chicago.

FIRST SPACE SHUTTLE FLIGHT

In April, America's first space shuttle, *Columbia*, makes its first flight, returning safely two days later. A second flight takes place in November.

AIDS IDENTIFIED

The U.S. Center for Disease Control identifies the first cases of what appears to be a new disease, AIDS (Acquired Immune Deficiency Syndrome). The condition affects a person's natural disease-combatting immune system and the first cases are identified in gay men.

RAIDERS OF THE LOST ARK

A new film, *Raiders of the Lost Ark*, is a great hit. It stars U.S. film actor Harrison Ford (b. 1942). He plays Indiana Jones, an archaeologist and man of action, who overcomes a bunch of Nazis hunting for the lost Ark of the Covenant. The film is full of spectacular effects.

BOB MARLEY (1945–1981)

Jamaican reggae artist Bob Marley (born Robert Nesta) has died of cancer. A Rastafarian, the singer and electric guitarist brought reggae to an international audience. Initially performing in a group of three known as the Wailers, Marley later went solo and gave performances worldwide. His latest album, *Uprising*, was produced last year. Among his best-known hits are *"No Woman No Cry"* and *"I Shot the Sheriff."*

EXPLORING THE SOLAR SYSTEM

Since the beginning of space exploration in 1961, sophisticated probes have been sent to explore the solar system and bring back photographs of our neighbors. More has been learned about our home system in the last 30 years than over previous millennia.

ABOVE LEFT: Jupiter photographed from *Voyager I* in 1979.

ABOVE RIGHT: A thin coating of ice on Mars, recorded by *Viking Lander 2*.

RIGHT: Photomosaic of Mercury assembled from photographs taken by *Mariner 10*.

LEFT: The innermost of Jupiter's 16 moons, seen from *Voyager I*.

BELOW LEFT: Venus, seen as a crescent, from *Pioneer Venus I*.

BELOW RIGHT: Saturn photographed by the probe *Voyager 2* in 1980.

ABOVE: Salman Rushdie, Bombay-born author of *Midnight's Children*, a novel about the partition of India. Later in the decade he will incur the wrath of Muslim leader Ayatollah Khomeini.

MIDNIGHT'S CHILDREN
British novelist Salman Rushdie (b. 1947) publishes an epic novel, *Midnight's Children*. Telling the stories of characters born at the moment of India's independence, the novel shows Rushdie to be one of Britain's foremost novelists.

HEART-LUNG TRANSPLANT IS SUCCESSFUL
In California, Mary D. Golkhe receives the first successful transplant of a heart and a pair of lungs. Three earlier recipients of heart-lung transplants lived only a few days.

ENTER THE PC
U.S. firm IBM introduces its personal computer (the PC), using the Microsoft Disk Operating System (MS-DOS). It becomes a standard program throughout the computer industry.

REDS
U.S. film actor Warren Beatty (b. 1937) stars in, co-writes, and directs a new movie. *Reds* is the story of John Reed, journalist and founding member of the American Communist party. The film is criticized for its disorganized structure, but is beautifully shot by Vittorio Storaro.

ABOVE: Dacca, Bangladesh, where President Zia ur-Rahman, leader of the Bangladesh Nationalist Party, is assassinated in May.

NEW MICROSCOPE
Physicists Gerd Binnig (b. 1947) of West Germany and Heinrich Roher of Switzerland invent the scanning tunneling microscope, which can identify individual atoms.

AUSTRIAN STATE RADIO REGIONAL STUDIO
In Austria, Gustav Peichl has designed a new radio studio that combines the economical use of prefabricated concrete sections with striking high-tech elements such as polished chromium heating pipes.

ANTI-APARTHEID PROTESTS
Serious anti-apartheid demonstrations disrupt the South African rugby tour of New Zealand, which has been nicknamed the "Barbed Wire Tour." Similar angry protests had met the South Africans visit to Great Britain in 1969.

CIVIL WAR IN LATIN AMERICA

Britain and Argentina go to war over ownership of the Falkland Islands. Israel drives the PLO out of Beirut and Christian Phalangists massacre Palestinian refugees. A state of emergency is declared in Nicaragua. Helmut Kohl becomes chancellor of Germany. The U.N. warns of destruction of the world's rain forests. Architecture adopts postmodernism, compact discs (CDs) appear on the market, and the U.S.S.R. puts a new space station into orbit.

1982

Mar	15	State of emergency is declared in Nicaragua
Apr	2	Argentinian troops invade Falkland Islands (Malvinas)
	19	U.S.S.R. puts a new space station into orbit
	26	British Royal Navy task force sets sail for Falklands
May	2	British submarine HMS *Conqueror* sinks Argentinian cruiser *General Belgrano*
	4	Argentinian missiles sink British destroyer HMS *Sheffield*
June	5	Israel invades Lebanon
	14	Argentinian forces surrender and the Falklands War ends
July	23	International Whaling Commission votes for complete ban on whaling

Aug	30	Yasser Arafat and Palestinians leave Beirut
Sep	18	Palestinians are massacred by Christian Phalangist militia in West Beirut
Oct	1	Helmut Kohl becomes the chancellor of West Germany
	28	Socialists win the election in Spain

LEFT: Helmut Kohl, the chancellor of West Germany.

FALKLANDS WAR

War breaks out between Argentina and Britain over ownership of the Falkland Islands. In April, the Argentinian junta under General Galtieri launches Operation Rosario and invades the Falkland Islands. The U.N. passes a resolution calling for Argentina to withdraw. A British task force is dispatched and, after a fierce conflict, Argentinian troops surrender and the islands are returned to Britain in June. Throughout the campaign, the British lose four warships and a container ship. They suffer 237 killed, as well as 18 civilians and 759 military personnel wounded. Argentina loses the battleship *Belgrano* and suffer more than 1,000 killed, including the crew of the *Belgrano*.

ISRAEL INVADES LEBANON

After an air bombardment, Israeli forces invade Lebanon, headquarters of the Palestinian Liberation Organization (PLO) since its formation in 1964. Israeli and Syrian forces clash in southern Lebanon and Israeli forces surround 6,000 PLO guerrillas in West Beirut and demand their surrender. In July, Palestinian leader Yasser Arafat (b. 1929) offers to accept a UN Security Resolution recognizing Israel's right to exist in exchange for U.S. recognition of the PLO, but the United States refuses. By the end of August, the PLO has been driven out of Beirut.

EL SALVADOR

Civil war continues in El Salvador where, in 1980, human rights champion Oscar Romero was killed. Elections take place, accompanied by considerable violence, with left-wing parties refusing to participate. The Christian Democratic Party, headed by José Duarte who has been president since 1980, is returned but is blocked by a coalition of right-wing parties.

ABOVE: A British Vulcan bomber plays its part in the Falklands conflict between Britain and Argentina.

PALESTINIANS MASSACRED

Following the assassination of Lebanese president-elect Bashir Gemayel, Christian Phalangists enter Palestinian refugee camps in West Beirut and kill more than 800 Palestinians.

SHINING PATH

In Peru, the Maoist guerrillas Sendero Luminoso (Shining Path), led by Dr. Renoso Guzman, become increasingly active by using terrorist tactics such as bombings and assassinations.

SOCIALISTS WIN IN SPAIN

In Spain, the Socialist Party of Felipe González (b. 1942) wins a landslide in the general election for the first time since the Civil War. He holds power until 1996.

INGRID BERGMAN
(1915–1982)

Swedish actress Ingrid Bergman has died. The English-speaking star (with Humphrey Bogart) of *Casablanca* (1942) had many other Hollywood successes during the 1940s. After a period in Europe, she returned to Hollywood in 1956 to make *Anastasia* and *The Inn of Sixth Happiness* (1958). More recently she appeared on stage and television and in Ingmar Bergman's film *Autumn Sonata* (1978).

ABOVE: Henry Fonda (with daughter Jane and Katharine Hepburn) wins his first and only Oscar for the film *On Golden Pond*.

KOHL BECOMES CHANCELLOR
The Social Democratic government of Helmut Schmidt falls. He is replaced as chancellor by the Christian Democrat Helmut Kohl (b. 1930), who holds power until 1998. Kohl does much to increase European unity in the EC and to bring France and Germany closer.

NEW SOVIET SPACE STATION
The Soviet Union puts a new space station into orbit. It is *Salyut 7*, which replaces an earlier space station that has been in orbit for four years.

NICARAGUA
President Daniel Ortega (b. 1945) declares a state of emergency in Nicaragua, following guerrilla attacks on bridges and petroleum installations. Relations with the United States have deteriorated since Reagan became president and U.S. aid to the country has been frozen since 1981. This year, the United States has begun actively attempting to destabilize the new Nicaraguan government by funding right-wing guerrillas known as Contras.

SOVIET LEADERS DIE
Soviet president Leonid Brezhnev dies, ushering in a period of weak leadership as two more leaders, Yuri Andropov and Konstantin Chernenko, both die within three years.

THE MARY ROSE IS RAISED
Archaeologists led by Margaret Rule raise the wreck of English king Henry VIII's warship, *Mary Rose*, off Portsmouth, England, after 437 years underwater.

SHUTTLE LAUNCHES SATELLITE
The U.S. space shuttle *Columbia* carries two communication satellites in its cargo bay and puts them into orbit. The shuttle carries two specialists, who are not astronauts, as additional crew members.

CDs ARRIVE
Compact discs (CDs), which store sound digitally as microscopic pits and play it back with a laser beam, go on sale along with the CD players. They are introduced by the Dutch company Philips and CBS/Sony of the United States.

FIRST LASER PRINTERS
The first laser printers for computers go on the market. They are manufactured by IBM.

POSTMODERN BUILDINGS
Designed by U.S. architect Michael Graves (b. 1934), the Portland Public Services Building in Oregon claims to be the first postmodern building. The colorful treatment of the facade, the play of patterns on the outer walls, and the use of ornamental statuary set this building apart from any other recent architectural project. A building in New York City, however, also claims to be postmodernism's "founding building." This is the AT&T Building designed by U.S. architects Philip Johnson and John Burgee. A highly controversial building, the skyscraper attracts immediate attention because of its enormous broken pediment, a historical allusion typical of the new style. It is nicknamed the "Chippendale skyscraper."

LEFT: The jubilant winning Italian soccer team raise the Jules Rimet trophy aloft after beating Germany to win the World Cup.

THE COLOR PURPLE

American writer Alice Walker (b. 1944) has published her first novel, *The Color Purple*. Walker's story of the life of an African-American woman will win her the Pulitzer Prize and international recognition.

THE HOUSE OF THE SPIRITS

Chilean writer Isabel Allende (b. 1942) gains international fame following the publication of her first novel, *The House of the Spirits*. A mixture of mythical elements and realism, the novel arose out of Allende's flight from Chile following the assassination of her uncle, Salvador Allende.

DESTRUCTION OF THE RAIN FOREST

Environmentalists are concerned about the state of the world's rain forests after a U.N. environment program estimates that some 20 million acres of rain forest are being destroyed annually.

PAC-MAN FEVER

The Pac-Man computer game sweeps America and Britain, becoming *Time* magazine's "Man of the Year."

ITALY WINS WORLD CUP

Italy wins the soccer World Cup for the third time at the final match staged in Spain. They beat Germany 3–1 in the final.

ABOVE: Russian premier Leonid Brezhnev dies and is buried in Moscow's Red Square. He is succeeded for a very short time by Yuri Andropov.

LEFT: Leader-in-waiting Mikhail Gorbachev; the death of Brezhnev begins the fall of the old guard and opens the way for the liberals to come to power in the Soviet Union.

WHALING MORATORIUM

The International Whaling Commission agrees to a four year moratorium on commercial whaling to begin 1985–1986. However, catches made for scientific research continue and much commercial whaling is disguised as "scientific."

CASA ROTONDA

Swiss-born architect Mario Botta's Casa Rotonda shows the flair of European architects for creating original forms. It is a cylindrically shaped house that plays inventively with volume.

GREENHAM WOMEN AND GERMAN GREENS

Civil war begins in Sri Lanka. A Soviet fighter shoots down a South Korean Boeing 747. Anti-nuclear protests take place throughout Europe against the siting of Cruise and Pershing missiles in Europe. German Greens win seats in the Bundestag. U.S. marines invade the island of Grenada. The AIDS virus is identified. A new device, the mouse, makes computer use easier. Steven Spielberg's film *ET*, starring a likeable extraterrestrial, becomes a smash hit.

OPPOSITE: Fiber optics are glass tubes which will revolutionize the telecommunications industry.

1983

Mar	**23**	U.S. president Reagan proposes a new "Star Wars" defense system
July	**27**	Civil war in Sri Lanka between government and Tamil Tigers
Aug	**21**	Philippines opposition leader Benigno Aquino is assassinated
Sept	**1**	Soviet fighter shoots down a South Korean Boeing 747
Oct	**20**	Speed of light is redefined
	23	A terrorist attack on U.S. Marine headquarters in Beirut kills 216 Marines
	25	United States invades Grenada
Nov	**28**	European *Spacelab* goes into orbit
Dec	**10**	Raul Alfonsín becomes president of Argentina

ABOVE: Boy George and his band Culture Club popularize gender-bending and cross-dressing across the westernized world.

U.S.S.R. SHOOTS DOWN BOEING

A South Korean Boeing 747 civilian aircraft, flying over Sakhalin Island off the east coast of Siberia, is shot down by Soviet pilots. The 269 passengers all lose their lives; the U.S.S.R. claims the plane was on a spying mission. The attack increases tension between the U.S.S.R. and the West.

ANTI-NUCLEAR PROTESTS

Large anti-nuclear demonstrations take place in many European countries against the placing of U.S. Cruise and Pershing II missiles in Europe. The missiles increase the number of nuclear warheads in Europe and add to the arms race between the United States and Soviet Union. In Britain, women set up a permanent peace camp on Greenham Common, where 96 cruise missiles are to be located. The women established the camp in September 1981 and maintain a constant vigil for peace.

GERMAN GREENS

The Green Party (die Grünen) wins a 5.6% share of the vote in national elections to the Bundestag, so achieving its first representation in the German legislative chamber. Among those to win a seat is Petra Kelly (1947–92), environmentalist, anti-nuclear activist and cofounder of the Green Party. Since the European Green Party was formed in 1979, concerns about the environment and nuclear power have led to increasing support across Europe.

MILITARY RULE ENDS IN ARGENTINA

Raul Alfonsín (b. 1927) becomes president of Argentina, ending eight years of military rule. The military's repressive measures affected all sections of society, but they have lost all authority since their defeat in the Falklands War in 1982.

UNITED STATES INVADES GRENADA

The presence of 1,000 U.S. students and a left-wing unelected government that had requested Cuban help with the construction of an international airport prompts the U.S. government to launch an invasion of the island of Grenada. Some 7,000 U.S. serviceman take two days to subdue a relatively untrained, ill-equipped and unsophisticated enemy. The Americans suffer 18 killed, 45 wounded; the Cubans 24 killed and 40 wounded; and the Grenadans 60 killed and 184 wounded.

MICE HELP KEYBOARDS

Apple Computer, Inc. introduces the computer mouse, a device that moves a pointer on screen and sends commands to the computer by the pressing of a button.

AQUINO ASSASSINATED

The opposition leader Benigno Aquino is assassinated at Manila airport as he returns from a three-year exile to fight the forthcoming general election. His death is widely blamed on the government of President Marcos, and fuels the opposition to his rule.

ABOVE: The Hummer or Humvee, a high-mobility multipurpose vehicle, replaces the faithful Jeep in the U.S. armed forces.

SRI LANKA

Civil war breaks out in Sri Lanka between government forces and northern Tamil separatists, the Liberation Tigers of Tamil Eelam (LTTE), based in the Jaffna peninsula. It continues into the 1990s.

AIDS VIRUS IDENTIFIED

Researchers in France discover the virus that causes AIDS. It is labeled HIV-1, the Human Immune Deficiency Virus; U.S. researchers confirm the finding the following year. There is some doubt about who is first to identify the virus but certainty that AIDS itself is likely to become an epidemic.

U.S. MARINES KILLED IN BEIRUT

216 U.S. Marines were killed when a truck loaded with over 2500 pounds of explosives drove through the security barriers and crashed into their headquarters.

FURTHER INTO SPACE

The European-built space laboratory *Spacelab* is put into orbit by the U.S. shuttle *Columbia*. In June, *Pioneer 10*, launched in 1972, becomes the first space probe to pass through the asteroid belt and travel beyond the solar system.

ET

U.S. filmmaker Steven Spielberg (b. 1946) releases a new film, *ET*. A delightfully sentimental tale of an alien who visits Earth, it becomes a major box-office earner. Much of the film is cleverly shot from the eye-level of the ten-year-old boy who is the central character.

WORST EL NINO

Oceanographers report that the El Niño spell of extra-warm water along the coast of South America, which began in 1982, is the most intense ever recorded. It causes floods and droughts in many parts of the world.

ABOVE: U.S. troops on the ground during the two day invasion of the tiny island of Grenada.

LEFT: The 82nd Airborne Division poised to land.

BELOW: A combined Marine and Army patrol during Operation Urgent Fury, the U.S. invasion of Grenada. The servicemen in the background are seated in a captured Soviet-built UAZ-469B light vehicle.

ADVANCES IN MEDICAL SCIENCE

Technological advances, partly developed for the space program, are successfully applied to the field of medicine. Computers, lasers, electronics, and nuclear science all take their place in diagnosis and surgical treatment.

RIGHT: Microsurgery uses powerful magnifying glasses, laser-guided instruments, and video screens for complex work.

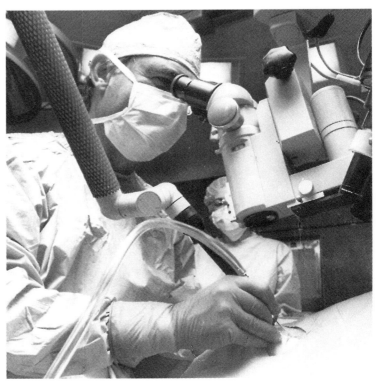

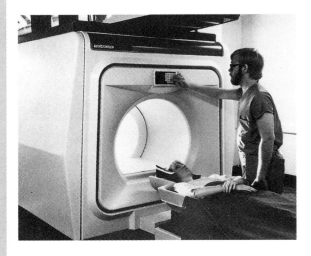

ABOVE: The Nuclear Magnetic Resonance Scanner is used to detect damage to, or cancers in, the bones and spine.

BELOW: Electrodes linked to a computer monitor the heart's rhythm and indicate any disruption to the patient's normal pattern.

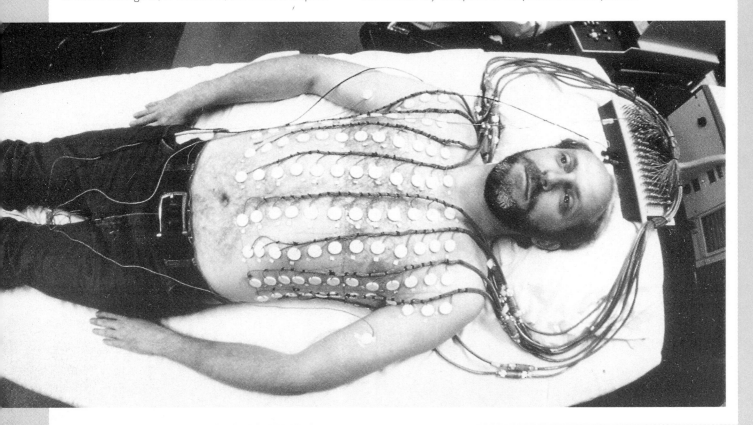

TALKING CAMERA
The Minolta Company introduces a 35mm camera which "talks" to the user, warning of problems before the next shot.

SPEED OF LIGHT REDEFINED
An international committee redefines the speed of light as exactly 983,571,000 feet per second.

FASHIONABLE GENDER-BENDING
Gender-bending, sexually indeterminate dressing and lifestyle, becomes a fashionable youth subculture in America and Britain with the success of rock bands such as Culture Club, led by a gay singer, Boy George.

ARTIFICIAL HEART
Retired dentist Barney B. Clark, the first patient to be given an artificial Jarvik heart, dies after 112 days. The artificial heart does not fail, but other organs do. The operation was carried out last year at the University of Utah. The artificial heart is made of plastic and metal and known as a Jarvik heart after its inventor, Robert Jarvik. It is to become useful as an interim measure while people wait for a suitable donor heart.

BALTHAZAR JOHANNES (JOHN) VORSTER
(1915–1983)

The Afrikaner Nationalist South African prime minister from 1966 to 1978, John Vorster, has died. He served as minister of justice during Hendrik Verwoerd's government (1961–1966) and became prime minister after the former's assassination, continuing to enforce apartheid. He was forced to resign his position as state president in 1979 when found guilty of misappropriation of government funds.

ABOVE: The remains of the barracks at Beirut Airport, where 241 U.S. Marines died in a terrorist bomb attack. The Marines are in Lebanon to help keep the peace between Israel and Palestine.

THE MASK OF ORPHEUS
British composer Harrison Birtwistle (b. 1934) retells the Orpheus myth in his new opera. As well as the traditional language of opera (voices and instruments), Birtwistle uses taped musical inserts of harp chords dissected, analyzed and replayed by a computer to create rhythms faster and more complex than a human player could achieve.

AUSTRALIA WINS AMERICA'S CUP
Australia wins the America's Cup from the United States for the first time since 1851. John Betterand captained the Australian yachting challenge in *Australia II*, defeating Dennis Conner's *Liberty*.

RIGHT: Everybody's favorite alien, ET the extraterrestrial, star of Spielberg's box office success, *ET*.

THE CHALLENGER ACHIEVEMENT

More than a decade after the first moonshot, the United States launches the space shuttle, a two-component vehicle comprising a rocket and an orbiter which can return to Earth. The first of the orbiters is the *Challenger*, launched in 1981 and in service until 1986. The idea is to carry out commercial, military, and scientific research. A major feature of the shuttle trips is the space walk, where astronauts leave the orbiter to carry out maintenance or construction work.

RIGHT: Astronauts F. Story Musgrave and Donald H. Peterson practice setting up a winch operation on the aft bulkhead.

BELOW: The astronauts spend almost four hours outside the *Challenger* as she orbits the Earth.

ABOVE: On a 1984 shuttle trip, astronaut Bruce McCandless II tests out the nitrogen-propelled, hand-controlled device called the Manned Maneuvering Unit (MMU), which allows great mobility. Previous spacewalkers were restricted by tethers, tying them to the mother ship.

LEFT: On a 1985 mission, astronauts Sherwood C. Spring and Jerry L. Ross practice the assembling of components outside the shuttle.

AMRITSAR, BHOPAL, AND ACID RAIN

Sikh nationalists are massacred at the Golden Temple, Amritsar. Indian prime minister Indira Gandhi is assassinated in revenge. In Britain, the IRA bombs the Conservative Party Conference as part of a sustained campaign to get British troops out of Northern Ireland. Nations in Ottawa pledge to reduce carbon dioxide emissions, the source of acid rain. In Bhopal, India, toxic gas kills more than 2,000. Women walk in space and Archbishop Tutu receives the Nobel Peace Prize.

1984

Feb	9	Soviet president Andropov dies. He is succeeded by Chernenko
	11	Iraq bombs nonmilitary targets in Iran
Apr	20	Demonstrations in West Germany against deployment of U.S. missiles in Europe
May	10	International Court of Justice at The Hague rules United States should end blockade of Nicaraguan ports
	10	Danish parliament votes to suspend payments to NATO as protest against siting of Pershing II and Cruise missiles in Europe
	24	Iranian warplanes attack oil tankers off coast of Saudi Arabia
June	6	Sikh nationalists killed when Indian troops storm Golden Temple, Amritsar
July	28	The 23rd Olympic Games open in Los Angeles
Aug	4	Tamils and Sinhalese clash in Sri Lanka
	25	Author Truman Capote dies at the age of 59
Sep	26	Britain agrees to hand over Hong Kong to China
Oct	12	IRA bombs Conservative Party Conference in Brighton, England
	31	Indian prime minister Indira Gandhi is assassinated
Nov	4	Sandanista Front wins the Nicaraguan elections
Dec	3	Toxic gas leak in Bhopal, India, kills and injures thousands

ABOVE: Mourners and the dead in Bhopal, the Indian city devastated by the leak of poisonous gas from the Union Carbide factory.

ABOVE: Ronald Reagan in Congress. The former actor has already served one term as president and this year is reelected for a second term.

LEFT: Indira Gandhi, the prime minister of India, with the Sikh bodyguard who later assassinates her.

GOLDEN TEMPLE MASSACRE

In June, members of the Sikh nationalist group the Akali Dal seize the Golden Temple, Amritsar, India, in an attempt to establish an independent Sikh state called Khalistan. The Golden Temple is one of the Sikhs' holiest places. The Indian government launches an attack and troops storm and seize the temple. Fighting is fierce: Official figures give 493 nationalists and 83 soldiers killed. In October, the Indian prime minister Indira Gandhi is assassinated by her Sikh bodyguards, in revenge for the storming of the Golden Temple. Mrs. Gandhi's son Rajiv (1944–1991) succeeds her to the premiership. The assassination provokes a Hindu backlash in which some 3,000 Sikhs are massacred.

BRIGHTON BOMBING

The IRA bomb the Conservative Party Conference in Brighton, England, narrowly avoiding killing prime minister Margaret Thatcher and her cabinet. Two people are killed and many injured in the blast, which wrecks the hotel they are staying in. The bomb is part of a sustained campaign by the IRA on the British mainland to force a British withdrawal from Northern Ireland.

FRANCOIS TRUFFAUT (1932–1984)

The *nouvelle vague* French film director and critic François Truffaut has died. His first full-length film *Les Quatre Cents Coups* (1959) immediately made his reputation and he consolidated this in 1962 with *Jules et Jim*. Many of his films form a loosely connected series featuring the actor Jean-Pierre Leaud, the boy hero of *Les Quatre Cents Coups*.

POISON GAS LEAK IN BHOPAL

Some 2,500 people are killed and thousands more injured when toxic gas escapes from the American-owned Union Carbide plant outside Bhopal, Madhya Pradesh, India. The leak is caused by the failure of two safety systems. Bhopal is declared a disaster zone.

BELOW: The blasted facade of the Grand Hotel, Brighton, where the IRA nearly succeeds in destroying the Conservative party.

ABOVE: The Anglo-French supersonic aircraft Concorde continues to fly the Atlantic in spite of protests by environmental activists.

HONG KONG TO BE RETURNED

Britain agrees to hand back Hong Kong to China in 1997. The 99 year lease on the New Territories runs out in 1997, making the rest of the colony unviable when they are returned to China. In the agreement, Hong Kong will be allowed to keep its capitalist system for at least 50 years and have considerable internal autonomy.

WALK IN SPACE

In June, Soviet cosmonaut Svetlana Savitskaya becomes the first woman to walk in space. She is followed in October by U.S. astronaut Kathryn D. Sullivan, who also walks in space.

FIRST CD-ROMS

Philips and Sony adapt the compact disc for computers, producing the first CD-ROMS (Compact Disc Read-Only Memory) for storing data.

OCEAN DRILLING

Eleven countries launch a ten year program of drilling to explore the continental shelves, parts of the continents that lie under the sea.

STAATSGALERIE EXTENSION

British architects James Stirling and Michael Wilford create their own muted version of postmodernism, with classical details and primary colors, for this art gallery extension in Stuttgart, Germany.

ACID RAIN PLEDGE

Ten nations meet in Ottawa and pledge to reduce sulphur dioxide emissions by 30 percent to reduce acid rain, which has been found to be contaminating lakes and rivers and destroying forests in much of North America and Europe. Only in 1983 was it discovered to be caused by pollutants in the smoke from power stations and some factories.

JORDAN SELECTED

The Chicago Bulls select Brooklyn-born Michael Jordan (b. 1963) third in the basketball draft of college players.

LINDOW MAN FOUND

The remains of an Iron Age man are discovered preserved in a peat bog at Lindow Marsh, Cheshire, England. He appears to have been the victim of a religious sacrifice.

OLYMPIC GAMES

The 23rd Olympics are held in Los Angeles. Many Communist countries boycott the games, which are the first to be privately financed, in retaliation for U.S. withdrawal in 1980. American sprinter Carl Lewis (b. 1961) achieves star status as he repeats Jesse Owens' haul of four golds. The women's marathon is an official Olympic event for the first time and is won by U.S. athlete Joan Benoit. Windsurfing, won by Holland's Stephen van den Berg, and synchronized swimming also become Olympic sports.

TUTU WINS NOBEL PRIZE

South African Anglican bishop and campaigner against apartheid Bishop Desmond Tutu (b. 1931) is awarded the Nobel Peace Prize. In 1985, he becomes the first black bishop of Johannesburg.

INDIRA PRIYAD ARSHINI GANDHI (1917–1984)

Indian prime minister Indira Gandhi has been assassinated by one of her guards. The daughter of Jawaharlal Nehru, she was educated partly at Oxford and was always politically active in the Congress party. She became prime minister in 1966 and lost her seat after a period of political upheaval in 1977. She was reelected in 1980.

PERESTROIKA AND LIVE AID

Mikhail Gorbachev becomes the new leader of the Soviet Union. He promises reforms. Ethiopia suffers the worst-ever recorded famine. Millions contribute to famine aid through massive Live Aid rock concerts. The Greenpeace ship *Rainbow Warrior* is sunk in New Zealand by French agents. The death of Rock Hudson stimulates awareness of the AIDS epidemic. Scientists discover a hole in the ozone layer. The wreck of the *Titanic* is found. English soccer clubs are banned from Europe competitions.

1985

Feb	10	ANC leader Nelson Mandela refuses offer of freedom, conditional on his renouncing violence
Mar	10	Soviet president Chernenko dies
	11	Mikhail Gorbachev becomes leader of the Soviet Union
	21	South African police fire on crowds on the 25th anniversary of the Sharpeville Massacre
Apr	11	Ramiz Alia becomes leader of Albania following the death of Enver Hoxha
May	1	United States imposes trade sanctions on Nicaragua
	15	Philadelphia police bomb the radical group Move and kill 11 people
	10	Sikh nationalists bomb Indian cities
July	11	Greenpeace ship *Rainbow Warrior* is sunk in Auckland, New Zealand

July	18	Organization of African Unity holds a conference in Addis Ababa; it announces that most African countries are on the verge of economic collapse
Sep	2	Pol Pot resigns as leader of Khmer Rouge
	17	More than 2,000 die after an earthquake in Mexico City
Oct	1	Israel attacks the PLO headquarters in Tunis
	2	U.S. film star Rock Hudson dies of AIDS
Nov	27	Anglo-Irish Agreement is signed giving the Republic of Ireland a consultative role in Northern Ireland
	29	Black union leaders form new trade union COSATU in South Africa

ABOVE: Tragedy in the Heysel Stadium, Brussels, as fans of soccer teams Liverpool and Juventus are crushed in a pre-match brawl.

GORBACHEV PROMISES REFORM

Following the death of Konstantin Chernenko, Mikhail Gorbachev (b. 1931) becomes leader of the Soviet Union. He begins to reform the Communist system, promising *glasnost* (openness) and *perestroika* (restructuring).

ALBANIA OPENS UP

Enver Hoxha, leader of Albania since 1945, dies. His country had been isolated from the rest of Eastern Europe, taking its lead from China rather than the U.S.S.R. It is the poorest country in Europe. Slowly, the new government of Ramiz Alia (b. 1925) begins to end Albania's international isolation.

ANGLO-IRISH AGREEMENT

British prime minister Margaret Thatcher and Irish prime minister Garret Fitzgerald (b. 1926) sign the Anglo-Irish Agreement, which gives Ireland a consultative role in the running of Northern Ireland for the first time. The agreement is designed to counter the campaign of the IRA and to begin the process of finding a solution to the long-running troubles in Northern Ireland.

ABOVE: Ruins in Mexico City after an earthquake hits the area this year. Over 2,000 people are killed.

LIVE AID

Mass famine in Ethiopia leads Irish rock star Bob Geldof (b. 1954) to organize Live Aid. Massive rock concerts are held in London and Philadelphia to raise money for famine relief. Stars, who play for free, include Dire Straits, David Bowie, Queen, and Mick Jagger. The concerts raise $60 million and do much to raise the world's consciousness about famine and poverty in Africa. The famine in Ethiopia, which began in 1981 after drought and prolonged civil war, is the world's worst as recorded last year by film cameramen.

GEORGE ORSON WELLES (1915–1985)

American film director and actor Orson Welles has died. His 1941 film *Citizen Kane*, in which he also starred, is greatly admired by film buffs. His other works include highly regarded films such as *The Magnificent Ambersons* (1942) and *Touch of Evil* (1958), both cut and amended by the studio without his consent. As an actor, Welles also leaves his famous performance as Harry Lime in *The Third Man* (1949). He will further be remembered for his panic-causing radio production of *War of the Worlds* in 1938.

KURDS ATTACK TURKEY

The Kurdistan Popular Liberation Army, formerly the Kurdish Worker's Party (PKK), begins military operations against the Turkish government.

RAINBOW WARRIOR SUNK

French secret agents sink the Greenpeace ship *Rainbow Warrior* in Auckland harbor, New Zealand. Environmental group Greenpeace sent the ship to the South Pacific to attempt to disrupt French nuclear tests on Mururoa Atoll, which are heavily criticized by all nations in the region.

OZONE HOLE DISCOVERED

Scientists of the British Antarctic Survey announce the discovery of a hole in the ozone layer over Antarctica. The discovery increases anxiety about global warming caused by carbon dioxide emissions.

AIDS EPIDEMIC

The World Health Organization (WHO) declares AIDS an epidemic. American film star Rock Hudson becomes the first celebrity to die of the disease, making people in the West more aware of its rapid spread.

BUCKYBALLS

U.S. chemist Richard E. Smalley makes new carbon molecules consisting of 60 atoms forming a hollow sphere. They are called buckminsterfullerenes, or buckyballs for short, after the inventor of the geodesic dome, R. Buckminster Fuller.

TITANIC LOCATED

Video cameras aboard an underwater search vessel locate the wreck of the liner *Titanic*, sunk in 1912, on the floor of the North Atlantic Ocean. The wreck is discovered off the Newfoundland coast in 13,200 feet of water.

GENETIC FINGERPRINTING

A team of British scientists led by Alec Jeffreys develops genetic fingerprinting, based on the fact that parts of the genetic code are unique to each person.

WOMEN'S RIGHTS

An international conference on women's rights takes place in Nairobi, Kenya; 10,000 women attend.

NATURAL DISASTERS

A massive earthquake hits Mexico City and kills 2,000. In Bangladesh, a cyclone and tidal wave kill 10,000.

YOUNG CHESS CHAMPION

The Russian Gary Kasparov (b. 1963) beats Anatoly Karpov (b. 1951), world champion and a fellow Russian, in one of the longest-running chess matches. He becomes the world's youngest chess champion.

RAN

Japanese film director Akira Kurosawa's *Ran* opens. A version of *King Lear* set in 16th century Japan, the film impresses audiences with its big battle scenes and strong characterization.

DEER FOR CHINA

Père David's deer, which became extinct in China in 1921, are sent to China from England, where they have been bred in captivity since 1894.

MARC CHAGALL
(1887–1985)

Little short of his centenary, the Russian-born Franco-Jewish painter Marc Chagall has died. He moved to France in 1922 and lived there for most of his life. He designed for the Ballets Russes and produced theatre posters, book illustrations and stained glass, as well as his many paintings. His style has been termed "fantastic art".

MAHABHARATA

English director Peter Brook (b. 1925) and French writer Jean-Claude Carrière (b. 1931) have produced a theatrical version of myths from the Hindu epic the *Mahabharata*. The production gains further recognition for Brook's Paris-based theatrical company, Les Bouffes du Nord.

ENGLISH SOCCER CLUBS BANNED

English soccer is devastated by two horrific events. In the northern town of Bradford, 56 die when an old wooden stand burns to the ground. Then at the European Cup Final between Liverpool and Juventus in the Heysel Stadium in Brussels, Belgium, 39 supporters of Turin club Juventus are crushed to death trying to get away from attacking Liverpool fans. English clubs are banned from European competitions and the tragedies force the English authorities to tackle hooliganism and the dilapidated state of English stadiums.

BELOW: The sinking hulk of *Rainbow Warrior*, the Greenpeace protest ship sunk in New Zealand by the French secret service.

STAR WARS

"Star Wars" is the nickname given to the Strategic Defense Initiative launched by President Ronald Reagan in 1983, which is to last as a research and development project for a decade. The plan is to devise a missile that can seek, catch, and destroy enemy missiles before they reach their target. Reagan sees it as the primary weapon in the battle against the "Evil Empire," his description of the Communist world.

LEFT: An artist's impression of a space-based nuclear power source to fuel the Star Wars missile, seen with its launcher, above.

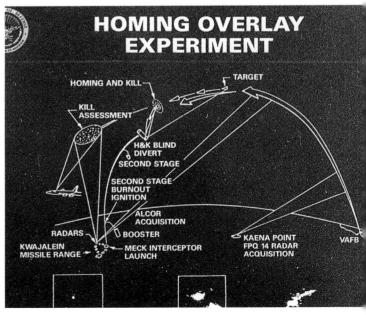

HOMING OVERLAY EXPERIMENT

HOMING AND KILL

KILL ASSESSMENT

TARGET

H&K BLIND DIVERT SECOND STAGE

SECOND STAGE BURNOUT IGNITION

ALCOR ACQUISITION

RADARS

BOOSTER

MECK INTERCEPTOR LAUNCH

KWAJALEIN MISSILE RANGE

KAENA POINT FPQ 14 RADAR ACQUISITION

VAFB

ABOVE: The tracker component of the project, which seeks and finds enemy intercontinental ballistic missiles.

ABOVE: Diagram to show how the Star Wars missiles would intercept the enemy and what ground support would be needed.

ABOVE: The Kill Mechanism of the Star Wars missile. A non-explosive "warhead," its metal ribs are wrapped around the neck of the defense missile during flight and unfurl seconds before impact. The force of the collision destroys the enemy missile.

RIGHT: The Airborne Optical Adjunct (AOA) is developed to optically identify and track warhead targets and to guide ground-based interceptors.

NUCLEAR EXPLOSION IN CHERNOBYL

A major nuclear accident occurs at Chernobyl in the Soviet Union. Radioactive gas spreads across Europe. U.S. space shuttle *Challenger* explodes seconds after takeoff. Mrs. Corazon Aquino topples Marcos in the Philippines. "Baby Doc" is overthrown in Haiti. The United States launches air strikes against Libya. New architectural landmarks include the Hong Kong Bank and Lloyds Building. Canadian author Margaret Atwood publishes a chilling feminist dystopia. Halley's Comet makes a return.

OPPOSITE: The space shuttle *Challenger* explodes on takeoff, killing all aboard.

1986

Jan	1	Spain and Portugal join the EC
	25	Gorbachev announces a 25 year plan for the elimination of nuclear weapons
	28	U.S. space shuttle *Challenger* explodes
Feb	7	Haitian president Jean-Claude Duvalier flees to France
	9	Halley's Comet makes closest approach to the Sun
	24	Marcos flees Philippines; Corazon Aquino sworn in as president
	28	Olaf Palme, Sweden's prime minister, is assassinated
Apr	11	Brian Keenan, lecturer in Beirut, is taken hostage
	15	U.S. bombers attack Libya from British bases
	17	John McCarthy, acting bureau chief for Worldwide Television, Beirut, is taken hostage
Apr	26	Major nuclear accident occurs at Chernobyl, Soviet Union
June	12	President Botha declares a state of emergency in South Africa
	20	Conference in Paris of 120 nations calls for sanctions against South Africa because of its apartheid policies
July	29	Argentina wins World Cup in Mexico
Aug	21	Toxic gas kills 1,700 in northern Cameroon
Sep	20	Israeli nuclear technician Mordechai Vanunu is kidnapped in London after revealing nuclear secrets.
Oct	19	President Machel of Mozambique and other government officials are killed in an air crash

ABOVE: The map used by Caspar Weinberger, Secretary of Defense, at a White House briefing to the U.S. Air Force during the Libyan action.

RIGHT: A Libyan patrol boat on guard in the Gulf of Sidra during the U.S. raids on Libya in retaliation for terrorist attacks on U.S. troops in mainland Europe.

JORGE LUIS BORGES
(1899–1986)

The highly regarded Argentine writer Jorge Luis Borges has died. His work consists mostly of essays or short narratives which engage the reader in the labyrinths of his complex metaphysical and multidimensional inventions. Because of increasing blindness he has dictated his ever-briefer essays since 1953. He was director of the Argentine National Library from 1955. The best-known collection of his works is *Labyrinths* (1962).

SIMONE DE BEAUVOIR
(1908–1986)

French writer and feminist Simone de Beauvoir, author of *The Second Sex*, has died. She was the fiercely independent companion of Jean-Paul Sartre and collaborated with him in producing the socialist paper *Les Temps Modernes* after the war. Her many published works contain novels and autobiographical writings including *Adieu: A Farewell to Sartre* (1984), about the last ten years of Sartre's life.

HAITIAN DICTATOR OVERTHROWN
The self-styled ruler for life of Haiti, Jean-Claude Duvalier, known as "Baby Doc," son of the dictator "Papa Doc," is toppled from power. Between them they have ruled the impoverished island since 1957, with the help of the dreaded Tonton Macoutes secret police. Duvalier flees to France, taking his considerable amount of loot with him. A military government takes over.

CHERNOBYL DISASTER
A nuclear power station at Chernobyl in Ukraine, Soviet Union, explodes causing a radioactive cloud to drift over northern Europe. Although a full meltdown and nuclear catastrophe are avoided, radioactive contamination in the area kills and maims many people. It is estimated that many thousands may die in the future due to radiation exposure.

STATE OF EMERGENCY IN SOUTH AFRICA
President Botha declares a state of emergency in South Africa as the government prepares for major anti-apartheid demonstrations on the tenth anniversary of the Soweto uprising. The move is criticized internationally and increases opposition to the white-only government among the black population.

EC MEMBERS
Spain and Portugal join the European Community as its 11th and 12th members.

UNITED STATES STRIKES LIBYA

Following the death of U.S. servicemen in a bomb attack on Berlin, the United States names Libya as responsible for the act and launch an air strike against Libya, destroying military installations around Tripoli and Benghazi. Some of the U.S. aircraft leave from British bases.

MACHEL KILLED

President Samora Machel of Mozambique and 28 government officials are killed in an air crash. South Africa is suspected, as part of its policy of destabilizing its black neighbors in order to weaken their opposition to the apartheid government.

CHALLENGER EXPLODES

The U.S. space shuttle *Challenger* explodes at Cape Canaveral just 73 seconds after takeoff. The explosion, which is seen by millions on television, kills all seven members of the crew and is the worst space disaster to date. Failure of rubber seals on a fuel line is blamed.

SPACE STATION MIR

The Soviet Union puts space station *Mir* into orbit around the Earth. It continues to function until the end of the century.

BELOW: The Chernobyl power station, three days after the worst nuclear accident the world has yet seen.

ABOVE: Mrs. Corazon Aquino (left) is sworn in as president of the Philippines. Her mother-in-law stands by her side.

HONG KONG BANK
British architect Norman Foster (b. 1935) designs a remarkable new building, the Hong Kong Bank. The structure is radical with the main elements supported on eight great masts and the floors hung from horizontal reinforcing struts. The structure is clearly visible from the outside, and gives the bank its distinctive lines.

AQUINO TAKES POWER IN PHILIPPINES
Mrs. Corazon Aquino (b. 1933), widow of the assassinated opposition leader, overthrows President Ferdinand Marcos. This follows mass demonstrations forcing him from office after he blatantly rigs the presidential election held in February.

LLOYD'S BUILDING
The new Lloyd's Building in London, designed by architect Richard Rogers, is dominated by its shining steel-clad stair towers and its vast 12 story glass hall. Brightly illuminated at night, the building becomes a new London landmark.

THE HANDMAID'S TALE
Canadian author Margaret Atwood (b. 1939) publishes a groundbreaking new novel. A feminist dystopia, it imagines a world in which fertile women become baby-producers for those who cannot have their own.

HALLEY'S COMET RETURNS
In February, Halley's Comet, returning after 76 years, makes its closest approach to the Sun. The space probe *Giotto* gets to within 373 miles of the nucleus and records valuable data.

LADY LIBERTY'S BIRTHDAY
The Statue of Liberty celebrated her 100th birthday on July 4 with President Reagan, warships, jet fighters, tall ships, and a spectacular fireworks display.

ARGENTINA WINS WORLD CUP
The 52 games of the Mexico soccer World Cup draw 2.5 million spectators to the stadiums. Argentina triumphs in the final with a 3–2 win over Germany.

NEWS FROM URANUS
Space probe *Voyager 2* flies close to Uranus and sends back pictures of the planet; it discovers two more rings and ten more moons.

BELOVED
A new novel by American author Toni Morrison (b. 1931) has been published. Entitled *Beloved*, it tells the true story of a runaway slave who kills her daughter when she is about to be recaptured, to save her from a life of slavery. It wins the author the Pulitzer Prize.

A "NEW" DINOSAUR
The fossilized bones of a previously unknown huge flesh-eating dinosaur are discovered by an amateur paleontologist, William Walker, in a clay pit in southern England.

ROUND THE WORLD NONSTOP
Pilots Richard D. Rutan and Jeana Yeager fly around the world nonstop without refueling, in *Voyager*, an experimental aircraft. The journey takes nine days.

PORTABLE PHONES
The first portable telephones appear. Although the size of a briefcase, they are an improvement on the first battery-operated cordless telephone of the late 1960s.

REFUGEES

Conflicts and unrest all over the world result in huge numbers of refugees. Governments, charities, and aid agencies have their work cut out to feed, shelter, and reestablish people uprooted by political, military, and climactic circumstances beyond their control.

LEFT: Afghani refugees in Iran collect water from a traditional irrigation system, the *khanat*.

ABOVE: "Boat people," refugees from South Vietnam, rescued from the South China Sea.

BELOW: An Afghani refugee in the settlement at Nazdasht, Iran, is able to maintain her pastoral way of life.

BELOW: Sumo and Miskito refugees being repatriated from Honduras (where they had fled in 1981) to Nicaragua.

ABOVE: Afghani refugees at Peshawar, Pakistan, sitting it out until they can return to their homeland.

U.S. AND U.S.S.R. END ARMS RACE

The United States and the Soviet Union sign a treaty agreeing to eliminate intermediate range nuclear weapons. British envoy Terry Waite is taken hostage in Beirut. Under the Montreal Protocol, 70 nations agree to limit the production of CFCs. Irangate causes a scandal in the United States. The U.N. begins a peace mission to end the Iran–Iraq war. Work begins on an Anglo-French Channel Tunnel. Van Gogh's painting *Irises* fetches an all-time record price.

OPPOSITE: The particle beam fusion accelerator, capable of generating 100 trillion watts of power.

1987

Jan	20	Archbishop's envoy Terry Waite is taken hostage in Beirut
Feb	5	Iran launches a missile attack on Baghdad, Iraq
	22	Artist Andy Warhol dies at age 55 following gall bladder surgery
	26	Tower Commission reports on Iran-Contra scandal
Mar	6	Cross-channel ferry capsizes off coast of Belgium
Apr	17	Tamils ambush buses in Sri Lanka
May	8	Leading Democratic presidential candidate Gary Hart withdraws from the race following allegations of sexual misconduct
	17	Iraqi Exocet missile hits USS *Stark* in Persian Gulf
Sep	11	U.N. Secretary General Pérez de Cuéllar begins a peace mission to end the Iran-Iraq war
Oct	16	Hurricane sweeps across southeast England, the worst storm in Britain for 300 years
Nov	2	Soviet leader Gorbachev criticizes Stalin in a speech marking the 70th anniversary of the Russian Revolution.
	8	IRA bombs explode at an Armistice Day parade in Enniskillen County Fermanagh, Northern Ireland. Eleven people are killed
Dec	7	INF Treaty is signed. U.S. president Reagan and Soviet leader Gorbachev agree to eliminate intermediate nuclear weapon

ABOVE: *Irises* by Vincent van Gogh (1853–1890) sells for $48 million. Art has now become an investment commodity.

WAITE TAKEN HOSTAGE
Terry Waite (b. 1939), a personal envoy of the Archbishop of Canterbury sent to Lebanon to negotiate the freedom of Western hostages in the country, is himself taken hostage by Hezbollah in Lebanon. Between 1983 and 1992, nearly 100 Westerners are grabbed off the streets of Beirut and held hostage for as long as seven years in guarded, underground cells throughout Lebanon.

IRANGATE
The profit from arms sent to Iran as part of a deal to free U.S. hostages in Lebanon is being used to support the right-wing Contra rebels fighting against the Nicaraguan government, contrary to the decision of U.S. Congress to stop supporting the Contras. The full extent of the Irangate conspiracy is revealed in the report of the Tower Commission set up to investigate the affair. The Tower Commission finds that President Reagan did not deliberately mislead the American people but seems to be unaware of important aspects of the operation.

INF TREATY
The Soviet Union and the United States sign an historic agreement to remove and dismantle all short and intermediate range nuclear weapons. The treaty requires the destruction of 1,752 Soviet and 859 U.S. missiles with ranges from 300 to 3,400 miles.

THE LAST EMPEROR
A new film by Italian Bernardo Bertolucci (b. 1940) has opened. *The Last Emperor* tells the story of the last Manchu ruler. A roaring success with both audiences and critics, it wins nine Oscars in 1988.

SCHINKELPLATZ
Architect Rob Krier uses a muted style, combining classical and traditional details, to produce housing in Berlin on a human scale to blend in with older buildings nearby.

TOP PRICE FOR IRISES
The painting *Irises* by Van Gogh fetches $48 million, a world record for art of all types. It confirms that he is the artist most in demand by international collectors. Three years later, in 1990, Van Gogh tops even this price when his *Portrait of Dr Gachet* fetches $80 million.

ZEEBRUGGE DISASTER
On March 6, a cross-channel ferry capsizes off Zeebrugge, Belgium, killing 187 people. It later transpires that the bow doors were left open.

COMPUTER COMPATIBILITY
Apple Computer, Inc. announces new Macintosh machines that can use software designed for the rival IBM machines.

ENTER SMART CARDS
A new type of credit card, the Smart Card, is introduced. It contains electronic chips, a tiny keyboard and display, and can process and store data.

CFC BAN AGREED

Seventy nations sign a protocol in Montreal to maintain use of CFCs (chlorofluorocarbons) at 1986 levels and to reduce levels in half by 1999. CFCs are believed to have caused a 90 percent thinning of the ozone layer over Antarctica. Ozone gas filters out harmful radiation from the Sun.

CHANNEL TUNNEL

Work on boring a tunnel under the English Channel between England and France begins on the English side. Work on the French side begins a year later.

A STAR EXPLODES

Astronomers in the southern hemisphere see a supernova (an exploding star) in a nearby galaxy.

USING GENETICS AGAINST CRIME

Genetic fingerprinting is first used in Britain to convict a criminal. The technique was developed in 1985 by Alec Jeffreys of the University of Leicester, who found that each person's core sequence of DNA is unique and can be used to determine family relationships.

DIGITAL TAPES

Digital audio tapes, which produce high-quality sound, go on sale. They are introduced by Aiwa in Japan.

RUGBY UNION

New Zealand wins the Webb Ellis Trophy in the inaugural Rugby Union World Cup, played in Australia and New Zealand. The All Blacks beat France 29–9 in the final of the 16-team event.

ANDY WARHOL
(1926–1987)

American artist and filmmaker Andy Warhol has died. One of the leading exponents of pop art, his early days as a commercial designer may have influenced his silk-screen produced repeated images of cans of soup and a photographic image of Marilyn Monroe. His avant-garde film factory in Greenwich Village produced works such as *Chelsea Girls* (1967). In 1968, his real life became much more eventful than his films when he was shot and seriously injured by the radical feminist Valerie Solanas.

FRED ASTAIRE
(1899–1987)

The inimitable American dancer, actor, and singer Fred Astaire (real name Frederick Austerlitz) has died. After 1920s Broadway successes with his sister Adele, he moved on to Hollywood when she married Lord Charles Cavendish. He had several dancing partners but the best-known was Ginger Rogers. They danced together with apparently effortless grace in *The Gay Divorcee* (1934), *Top Hat* (1935), *Swing Time* (1936), and seven others. Despite his "retirement" in 1946 he continued to make musicals and to act on screen until the late 1970s.

BUSH AND BHUTTO COME TO POWER

Ethnic and regional unrest begins in the Baltic states. Chilean dictator Pinochet steps down, clearing the way for democracy to return to Chile. A terrorist bomb explodes on a jumbo jet over Lockerbie, Scotland. The United States shoots down an Iranian airbus by accident. Drugs dominate the Seoul Olympics. Benazir Bhutto becomes the first Islamic woman prime minister. U.S. climatologist warns that the "greenhouse effect" has begun.

OPPOSITE: Benazir Bhutto, the first woman prime minister of Pakistan.

1988

Jan	26	Australia celebrates the 200th anniversary of the arrival of white settlers. Aborigines hold protests and declare it a time of mourning
Feb	13	The Winter Olympics begin in Calgary, Canada
Mar	13	Seikan Tunnel opens, linking islands of Honshu and Hokkaido, Japan
May	13	Soviet troops begin their withdrawal from Afghanistan
July	3	USS *Vincennes* shoots down an Iranian airbus
	6	Oil rig Piper Alpha explodes, killing 290 people
	18	Nelson Mandela's 70th birthday; the event is marked by worldwide calls for his release
Aug	8	Iran-Iraq cease-fire ends eight years of war
Sep	17	Olympic Games open in Seoul, South Korea
Oct	3	Chad and Libya formally end war that has been going on since 1965
	6	Chilean dictator General Pinochet steps down after losing referendum
Nov	8	Republican George H.W. Bush wins U.S. presidential elections
	16	Estonian parliament votes to give itself rights to veto laws from Moscow
Dec	2	Benazir Bhutto is sworn in as prime minister of Pakistan
	7	Soviet leader Mikhail Gorbachev announces plans to reduce Red Army
	21	Pan Am Flight 103 jumbo jet is blown up over Lockerbie, Scotland

UNREST IN BALTIC STATES

Ethnic and regional unrest grows in the Baltic states and Georgia as Gorbachev tries to reform the Soviet Union without breaking it up. Discontent with economic failure and lack of civil liberties leads to growing unrest and demands for autonomy and even independence from the 15 republics of the U.S.S.R.. In December, Gorbachev announces huge unilateral cuts in the Red Army, including massive reductions in the armies kept in Eastern Europe.

PINOCHET STEPS DOWN

The Chilean military dictator General Pinochet (b. 1915) loses a referendum on democracy and steps down after 15 years in power. During his presidency, 3,000 people have been assassinated, 1,000 "disappeared," 200,000 tortured, and an additional 5,000–6,000 victims may have been buried in unmarked graves. In December 1989, Patricio Aylwin Azócar is elected president and democracy is restored to Chile, with Pinochet gaining immunity for life.

BUSH BECOMES PRESIDENT

George Bush, vice president for eight years, wins the U.S. presidential election and continues Reaganomic policies.

ABOVE: An earthquake devastates Armenia.

LOCKERBIE DISASTER

In December, Pan Am Flight 103 crashes after a terrorist bomb detonates over Lockerbie, Scotland. All 259 passengers die when the 747 crashes and 11 inhabitants of Lockerbie are killed by wreckage. Evidence points to Libya and two intelligence officers are suspected. Libya refuses to give them up and U.N. sanctions are imposed. In 1999, the two will be flown to Holland to be tried under Scottish law.

IRANIAN AIRBUS SHOT DOWN BY MISTAKE

The USS *Vincennes* shoots down an Iranian airbus by mistake, killing all 290 passengers. Following the Iraqi Exocet air attack, directed at oil tankers en route to Iran which severely damaged the USS *Stark* in 1987, U.S. Navy warships in the Gulf have been on high alert. The Aegis automatic air defense system on the *Vincennes* picked up an aircraft, identified it as hostile, and shot it down mistakenly.

GREENHOUSE EFFECT

U.S. climatologist James E. Hansen predicts that the "greenhouse effect" in which a buildup of carbon dioxide in the atmosphere traps heat at the Earth's surface, has begun.

HUMAN GENOME PROJECT

A research scheme called the Human Genome Project begins. It plans to map the complete sequence of nucleic acids in human DNA.

LEFT: Vice President George Bush and his wife Barbara hit the campaign trail in California on their way to the White House.

ENVIRONMENTALIST MURDERED

Brazilian environmentalist and labor leader Chico Mendez is assassinated by a cattle rancher. Mendez had been actively campaigning against the destruction of the Brazilian rain forests and had unionized itinerant rubber tappers (rubber tapping being a sustainable use of the rain forest). In 1987, he was awarded a U.N. ecology prize but had received many death threats.

SEIKAN TUNNEL COMPLETED

The Seikan Rail Tunnel connecting the Japanese islands of Honshu and Hokkaido is opened after 24 years of work. At nearly 34 miles long, it is the world's longest tunnel. It is also the final stage in the project to link Japan's four islands by train.

WOMAN MUSLIM LEADER

Benazir Bhutto (b. 1953), leader of the democratic Pakistan People's Party, is elected as Pakistan's prime minister. She is the first modern-day woman to be leader of a Muslim country.

MONTAG AUS LICHT

For years, German composer Karlheinz Stockhausen (b. 1928) has been engaged on a self-proclaimed masterpiece, a vast cycle of seven operas (one for each day of the week), known collectively as *Licht* ("light"). Now he has completed Monday.

WINTER OLYMPICS

Calgary in the Canadian Rockies is the venue for the 15th Winter Olympics, which have been extended from 12 to 16 days. Italian skier Alberto Tomba (b. 1966) wins two skiing golds and German ice skater Katarina Witt (b. 1965) becomes only the second woman to win back-to-back figure skating crowns.

ABOVE: Official investigators comb the wreckage of Pan Am Flight 103, which was blown up over the Scottish town of Lockerbie.

FIRST WOMAN BISHOP

Barbara Harris (b. 1930), a black woman priest, is elected the first woman bishop in the Anglican communion. She will serve as the suffragan bishop of Massachusetts.

FOSSIL BIRD

Spanish scientists report the discovery of a previously unknown fossil of a bird which lived about 125 million years ago. It appears to be a link between the earliest known bird, *Archaeopteryx*, and modern birds.

FAKE SHROUD

A fragment of cloth from the Turin Shroud, believed to be the winding sheet of Jesus, is given a radiocarbon test that shows it was probably made no earlier than 1350.

AIR SHOW TRAGEDY

46 spectators were killed by falling debris when 3 jets collided in mid-air during an air show at Ramstein Air Base south of Frankfurt, Germany.

SEOUL OLYMPICS

Drugs dominate the 24th Olympic Games in Seoul, South Korea. Ben Johnson claims the 100m gold in a world record 9.79 seconds, but the Canadian is stripped of both medal and record when he fails a test for banned drugs. Known for her fashion sense and painted nails, American sprinter Florence Griffith-Joyner (Flo-Jo) shows she is a true champion, winning three golds and a silver. She dies tragically young in 1998.

THE END OF COMMUNIST RULE

The Cold War finally comes to an end as the Berlin Wall comes down, uniting West and East Germany. Eastern European countries, Hungary, Poland, Romania, and Czechoslovakia, move decisively away from Communist control. The last Soviet troops leave Afghanistan and the Angolan civil war comes to an end after 14 years of fighting. In China, troops suppress the prodemocracy movement. U.S. troops invade Panama. The Ayatollah issues a fatwa against author Salman Rushdie.

1989

Jan	10	Cuban troops begin withdrawal from Angola
Feb	2	South African president Botha resigns; he is succeeded by F.W. de Klerk
	3	Military coup overthrows the 35 year dictatorship of President Alfredo Stroessner in Paraguay
	14	Ayatollah Khomeini issues a fatwa against author Salman Rushdie
	15	Last Soviet troops leave Afghanistan after ten years
Mar	24	Oil tanker *Exxon Valdez* runs aground, causing a massive oil spill
Apr	17	In China, students call for democracy and march on Tiananmen Square
	20	Multiparty elections are held in Czechoslovakia for the first time since 1946
June	4	Solidarity candidates defeat the Communists in Polish elections I
	23	Angolan president dos Santos and UNITA leader Savimbi sign declaration ending civil war
Sep	10	Hungary opens its borders for East Germans
	12	New Polish government is the first in Eastern Europe not under Communist rule since 1946
	26	Last of 50,000 Vietnamese forces leave Cambodia
Oct	19	Earthquake hits California
Nov	10	Berlin Wall demolished
Dec	19	U.S. troops invade Panama to overthrow General Noriega
	30	Romanian dictator Nicolae Ceausescu executed

PARAGUAYAN DICTATORSHIP ENDS

General Alfredo Stroessner, ruler of Paraguay, is overthrown in a coup after 35 years in power. He is replaced by General Andrés Rodríguez, who wins the presidential election held in May. The fall of Stroessner removes the longest-standing military dictatorship in South America.

AYATOLLAH ISSUES FATWA

In Iran, Ayatollah Khomeini issues a fatwa or death threat against Salman Rushdie, the British author of *The Satanic Verses*, because of the book's supposed blasphemous content. Rushdie goes into hiding, only emerging cautiously when the threat is partly lifted in September 1998.

POLAND ADOPTS NON-COMMUNIST GOVERNMENT

Polish trade union Solidarity is legalized after talks between its leader, Lech Walesa, and the government. The Catholic Church is given a status unprecedented in Europe and Poland begins to move towards multiparty democracy. In August, the Solidarity candidate Tadeusz Mazowiecki is elected prime minister as the Communist General Jaruzelski (b. 1923) remains president. The new government is the first non-Communist government in Eastern Europe since the late 1940s.

HUNGARY OPENS BORDERS

The Hungarian Army dismantles the border fence with Austria as a symbol of the strengthening democratic reforms in the country. When the border posts are opened in September, many East Germans take the opportunity to flee to the West across Hungary's open borders.

COMMUNISM COLLAPSES

Hungary becomes a multiparty democracy as the Communist party gives up power and changes its name and ideology. In the same month, the East German government collapses after mass demonstrations in the major cities led by the New Forum, a democratic pressure group calling for reform.

BERLIN WALL FALLS

In November, the government opens East Germany's borders and demolishes the wall separating East and West Berlin, uniting the city divided since 1945. In both Bulgaria and Czechoslovakia, the Communist party renounces its monopoly on power as both governments fall. In December, the playwright Vaclav Havel (b. 1936) wins the election as the first non-Communist president of Czechoslovakia since 1948.

SAN FRANCISCO EARTHQUAKE

An earthquake caused by the San Andreas Fault strikes San Francisco and Oakland, California, killing 62 people and causing widespread damage and fires.

CEAUSESCU EXECUTED

Street fighting breaks out in Bucharest as the Committee for National Salvation, backed by the Army, attacks buildings held by the state secret police, the Securitate. Romanian dictator Nicolae Ceausescu and his wife flee Bucharest. They are swiftly recaptured and killed by a firing squad on Christmas Day for "crimes against the people." The Romanian Communist Party is abolished and the ruling National Salvation Front promises free elections as the country moves towards democracy.

OPERATION JUST CAUSE

Some 12,000 U.S. troops invade Panama to oust General Manuel Noriega who has become implicated with Central American drug dealers as well as with human rights abuses. In the fighting, 220 Panamanians and 314 soldiers are killed. The American forces suffer 23 dead and 324 wounded. Three civilians are killed.

STUDENTS KILLED IN TIANANMEN SQUARE

Students and other prodemocracy protesters occupying Tiananmen Square in Beijing, China, are fired on by the Red Army as it reoccupies the square. Many hundreds are killed and thousands later imprisoned as the pro-democracy movement is suppressed throughout China.

SOVIETS WITHDRAW FROM AFGHANISTAN

The last Soviet troops leave Afghanistan after a ten year occupation. The long drawn-out guerrilla war has cost the U.S.S.R. more than 15,000 killed, 311 missing, and 35,478 wounded. The Afghans lose over 100,000 killed.

THE PROTECTING VEIL

This new cello piece by British composer John Tavener (b. 1944) is hailed as a powerful example of the "new simplicity" in music. Its spiritual content makes it popular and it goes to the top of the CD charts.

CLOSE-UP OF NEPTUNE

Space probe *Voyager 2* passes within 3,106 miles of Neptune after a journey of more than 12 years, sending back clear pictures and discovering a Great Dark Spot and fierce winds.

IVORY TRADE BANNED

The Convention on International Trade in Endangered Species agrees to a total ban on trading in ivory. In Kenya, 12 tons of elephant tusks are burnt as a sign of commitment to stamping out the trade.

ECSTASY FUELS RAVE SCENE

The development of the rave scene youth subculture is fueled by the drug ecstasy and techno dance music. Tens of thousands of teenagers and people in their 20s are attracted to acid-house rave parties.

ABOVE: Batman, the caped crusader, in a somber mood amid props and sets reminiscent of the dystopian *Metropolis*.

LEFT: Unrest in middle America as the downside of Reaganomics strikes home, just after their champion leaves office.

BELOW LEFT: Somalian refugees at the Hartisheik camp in Ethiopia make do with whatever is at hand to make a home.

OPPOSITE: After almost 30 years, the Berlin Wall comes down as the Eastern bloc crumbles and the Cold War finally ends.

BATMAN
American star Michael Keaton's portrayal of the caped crusader is more brooding than the lighthearted version of earlier cartoons and films; this is helped by the sets and props. This new version of Batman breaks box office records within months of opening.

HILLSBOROUGH SOCCER DISASTER
Overcrowding kills 95 Liverpool fans at an F.A. Cup semifinal at Hillsborough in Sheffield, U.K. It is the highest death toll in British sports history and forces further reform of the game.

JIM BAKKER JAILED
Former televangelist Jim Bakker was sentenced to 45 years in prison for fraud and conspiracy charges related to his PTL ministry and Heritage USA Christian park.

EXXON VALDEZ OIL DISASTER

The *Exxon Valdez* oil tanker runs aground in Prince William Sound, Alaska. Almost 11 million gallons of crude oil spills into the sea and spreads over 900 square miles of coast, devastating marine life.

RIGHT: A boom is used to try and scrape surface oil off the water.

BELOW: The cleanup team moves in to assess the damage to the coastline and plan a strategy for remediation.

ABOVE: A golden-eye duck, one of the innocent victims of the spill.

ABOVE: Aerial view of the huge extent of the damage.

WINNERS AND ACHIEVERS OF THE 1980s

ACADEMY AWARDS

The Academy of Motion Picture Arts and Sciences was founded in 1927 by the movie industry to honor its artists and craftsmen. All categories of motion picture endeavor are honored, but the most significant are listed below.

BEST ACTOR

1980 Robert De Niro *Raging Bull*
1981 Henry Fonda *On Golden Pond*
1982 Ben Kingsley *Gandhi*
1983 Robert Duvall *Tender Mercies*
1984 F. Murray Abraham *Amadeus*
1985 William Hurt *Kiss of the Spider Woman*
1986 Paul Newman *The Color of Money*
1987 Michael Douglas *Wall Street*
1988 Dustin Hoffman *Rain Man*
1989 Daniel Day-Lewis *My Left Foot*

BEST ACTRESS

1980 Sissy Spacek *Coal Miner's Daughter*
1981 Katharine Hepburn *On Golden Pond*
1982 Meryl Streep *Sophie's Choice*
1983 Shirley MacLaine *Terms of Endearment*
1984 Sally Field *Places in the Heart*
1985 Geraldine Page *The Trip to Bountiful*
1986 Marlee Matlin *Children of a Lesser God*
1987 Cher *Moonstruck*
1988 Jodie Foster *The Accused*
1989 Jessica Tandy *Driving Miss Daisy*

BEST DIRECTOR

1980 Robert Redford *Ordinary People*
1981 Warren Beatty *Reds*
1982 Sir Richard Attenborough *Gandhi*
1983 James L. Brooks *Terms of Endearment*
1984 Milos Forman *Amadeus*
1985 Sydney Pollack *Out of Africa*
1986 Oliver Stone *Platoon*
1987 Bernardo Bertolucci *The Last Emperor*
1988 Barry Levinson *Rain Man*
1989 Oliver Stone *Born on the Fourth of July*

BEST PICTURE

1980 *Ordinary People*
1981 *Chariots of Fire*
1982 *Gandhi*
1983 *Terms of Endearment*
1984 *Amadeus*
1985 *Out of Africa*
1986 *Platoon*
1987 *The Last Emperor*
1988 *Rain Man*
1989 *Driving Miss Daisy*

NOBEL PRIZES

The Nobel Prizes are an international award granted in the fields of literature, physics, chemistry, physiology or medicine, and peace. The first prizes were awarded in 1901 and funded by the money left in the will of the Swedish inventor Alfred Nobel (1833–1896), who gave the world dynamite.

PRIZES FOR LITERATURE

1980 Czeslaw Milosz (Polish) for poetry
1981 Elias Canetti (Bulgarian-born) for fiction and non-fiction.
1982 Gabriel Garcia Marquez (Colombian) for fiction
1983 William Golding (British) for fiction
1984 Jaroslav Seifert (Czech) for poetry
1985 Claude Simon (French) for fiction
1986 Wole Soyinka (Nigerian) for drama, poetry and fiction
1987 Joseph Brodsky (Soviet-born) for poetry
1988 Najib Mahfuz (Egyptian) for fiction
1989 Camilo José Cela (Spanish) for fiction

PRIZES FOR PEACE

1980 Adolfo Perez Esquivel (Argentine) for activities in Service for Peace and Justice in Latin America, a group promoting the cause of human rights
1981 Office of the United Nations High Commissioner for Refugees for the protection of millions of Vietnamese and other refugees
1982 Alva Myrdal (Swedish) and Alfonso Garcia Robles (Mexican) for contributions to United Nations disarmament negotiations
1983 Lech Walesa (Polish) for efforts to prevent violence while trying to gain workers' rights
1984 Desmond Tutu (South African) for leading a non-violent campaign against ethnic segregation in his country
1985 International Physicians for the Prevention of Nuclear War for educating the public on the effects of nuclear war
1986 Elie Wiesel (American) for efforts to help victims of oppression and racial discrimination
1987 Oscar Arias Sanchez (Costa Rican) for authoring a plan to end civil wars in Central America
1988 U.N. peacekeeping forces for controlling military conflict
1989 Dalai Lama (Tibetan) for non-violent struggle to end China's rule of Tibet.

PRIZES FOR PHYSICS

1980 James Cronin and Val Fitch (American) for research on subatomic particles revealing that the fundamental laws of symmetry in nature could be violated
1981 Nicolaas Bloembergen and Arthur Schawlow (American) for contributions to the development of laser spectroscopy, and Kai Siegbahn (Swedish) for contributions to the development of high-resolution electron spectroscopy
1982 Kenneth Wilson (American) for the method of analysing the behaviour of matter when it changes form
1983 Subrahmanyan Chandrasekhar and William Fowler (American) for work on the evolution and death of stars
1984 Carlo Rubbia (Italian) and Simon van der Meer (Dutch) for contributions to the discovery of two subatomic particles — the W and the Z particles
1985 Klaus von Klitzing (West German) for developing a precise way of measuring electrical resistance
1986 Ernst Ruska (West German) for the invention of the electron microscope and Gerd Binnig (West German) and Heinrich Rohrer (Swiss) for the invention of the scanning tunnelling microscope
1987 J. George Bednorz (West German) and K. Alex Muller (Swiss) for the discovery of superconductivity in a ceramic material
1988 Leon Lederman, Melvin Schwartz and Jack Steinberger (American) for work on neutrinos
1989 Hans G. Dehmelt (American) and Wolfgang Paul (German) for isolating and measuring single atoms, and Norman Ramsey (American) for work that led to the development of the atomic clock

PRIZES FOR CHEMISTRY

1980 Paul Berg and Walter Gilbert (American) and Frederick Sanger (British) for studies of the chemical structure of nucleic acids
1981 Kenichi Fukui (Japanese) and Roald Hoffman (American) for applying the theories of quantum mechanics to predict the course of chemical reactions
1982 Aaron Klug (South African-born) for work with the electron microscope and for research into the structure of nucleic acid-protein complexes
1983 Henry Taube (American) for research on electron transfer between molecules in chemical reactions
1984 R. Bruce Merrifield (American) for developing a method to make peptides
1985 Herbert A. Hauptman and Jerome Karle (American) for techniques to quickly determine the chemical structure of molecules vital to life

WINNERS AND ACHIEVERS OF THE 1980s

1986 Dudley Herschbach and Yuan Lee (American) and John Polanyi (Canadian) for work on chemical reactions
1987 Jean-Marie Lehn (French) and Donald Cram and Charles Pederson (American) for work on artificial molecules
1988 Johann Deisenhofer, Robert Huber and Hartmut Michel (West German) for revealing the structure of proteins that are essential to photosynthesis
1989 Sidney Altman and Thomas Cech (American) for the discovery that RNA (ribonucleic acid) can aid chemical reactions in cells

PRIZES FOR PHYSIOLOGY OR MEDICINE

1980 Baruj Benacerraf and George D. Snell (American) and Jean Dausset (French) for discoveries about the genetic regulation of the body's immune system
1981 Roger W. Sperry and David H. Hubel (American) and Torsten Wiesel (Swedish) for research on the organization and functioning of the brain
1982 Sune Bergstrom and Bengt Samuelsson (Swedish) and John Vane (British) for discoveries regarding prostaglandins and related substances
1983 Barbara McClintock (American) for the discovery that genes sometimes behave unexpectedly inside cells.
1984 Niels Jerne (British), Georges Kohler (German) and Cesar Milstein (Argentine) for discoveries in immunology
1985 Michael S. Brown and Joseph L.. Goldstein (American) for explaining how high cholesterol levels in the blood cause heart disease
1986 Stanley Cohen (American) and Rita Levi-Montalcini (Italian-born) for research on cell and organ growth

1987 Susumu Tonegawa (Japanese) for discovering how genes produce antibodies against specific disease agents.
1988 Gertrude B. Elion and George H. Hitchings (American) and Sir James Black (British) for discoveries of important principles of drug treatment
1989 J. Michael Bishop and Harold E. Varmus (American) for research on cancer-causing genes called oncogenes

INDIANAPOLIS 500 WINNERS

1980 Johnny Rutherford
1981 Bobby Unser
1982 Gordon Johncock
1983 Tom Sneva
1984 Rick Mears
1985 Danny Sullivan
1986 Bobby Rahal
1987 Al Unser
1988 Rick Mears
1989 Emerson Fittipaldi

KENTUCKY DERBY WINNERS

1980 Genuine Risk
1981 Pleasant Colony
1982 Gato del Sol
1983 Sunny's Halo
1984 Swale
1985 Spend a Buck
1986 Ferdinand
1987 Alysheba
1988 Winning Colors
1989 Sunday Silence

NBA CHAMPIONS

1980 Los Angeles Lakers defeat Philadelphia 76ers
1981 Boston Celtics defeat Houston Rockets
1982 Los Angeles Lakers defeat Philadelphia 76ers
1983 Philadelphia 76ers defeat Los Angeles Lakers
1984 Boston Celtics defeat Los Angeles Lakers
1985 Los Angeles Lakers defeat Boston Celtics

1986 Boston Celtics defeat Houston Rockets
1987 Los Angeles Lakers defeat Boston Celtics
1988 Los Angeles Lakers defeat Detroit Pistons
1989 Detroit Pistons defeat Los Angeles Lakers

SITES OF THE OLYMPIC GAMES

1980 SUMMER Moscow, Soviet Union
WINTER Lake Placid, USA
1984 SUMMER Los Angeles, USA
WINTER Sarajevo, Yugoslavia
1988 SUMMER Seoul, South Korea
WINTER Calgary, Canada

U.S. PRESIDENTS

1977–1981 President James Earl Carter, Democrat
1977–1981 Vice President Walter F. Mondale
1981–1989 President Ronald Reagan, Republican
1981–1989 Vice President George H.W. Bush
1989–1993 President George H.W. Bush, Republican
1989–1993 Vice President Dan Quayle

SUPER BOWL CHAMPIONS

1980 Pittsburgh Steelers defeat Los Angeles Rams
1981 Oakland Raiders defeat Philadelphia Eagles
1982 San Francisco 49ers defeat Cincinnati Bengals
1983 Washington Redskins defeat Miami Dolphins
1984 L.A. Raiders defeat Washington Redskins
1985 San Francisco 49ers defeat Miami Dolphins
1986 Chicago Bears defeat New England Patriots
1987 New York Giants defeat Denver Broncos
1988 Washington Redskins defeat Denver Broncos
1989 San Francisco 49ers defeat Cincinnati Bengals

WORLD CUP FINAL MATCHES

YEAR LOCATION
1982 Madrid
Italy defeats West Germany 3-1
1986 Mexico City
Argentina defeats West Germany 3-2

WIMBLEDON CHAMPIONS

1980 MEN Bjorn Borg
WOMEN Evonne Goolagong Cawley
1981 MEN John McEnroe
WOMEN Chris Evert Lloyd
1982 MEN Jimmy Connors
WOMEN Martina Navratilova
1983 MEN John McEnroe
WOMEN Martina Navratilova
1984 MEN John McEnroe
WOMEN Martina Navratilova
1985 MEN Boris Becker
WOMEN Martina Navratilova
1986 MEN Boris Becker
WOMEN Martina Navratilova
1987 MEN Pat Cash
WOMEN Martina Navratilova
1988 MEN Stefan Edberg
WOMEN Steffi Graf
1989 MEN Boris Becker
WOMEN Steffi Graf

WORLD SERIES CHAMPIONS

1980 Philadelphia Phillies defeat Kansas City Royals
1981 Los Angeles Dodgers defeat New York Yankees
1982 St. Louis Cardinals defeat Milwaukee Brewers
1983 Baltimore Orioles defeat Philadelphia Phillies
1984 Detroit Tigers defeat San Diego Padres
1985 Kansas City Royals defeat St. Louis Cardinals
1986 New York Mets defeat Boston Red Sox
1987 Minnesota Twins defeat St. Louis Cardinals
1988 Los Angeles Dodgers defeat Oakland Athletics
1989 San Francisco Giants defeat Oakland Athletics